Learning to Govern

LEARNING TO GOVERN

An Institutional View
of the 104th Congress

Richard F. Fenno Jr.

BROOKINGS INSTITUTION PRESS
Washington, D.C.

About Brookings

The Brookings Institution is a private nonprofit organization devoted to research, education, and publication on important issues of domestic and foreign policy. Its principal purpose is to bring knowledge to bear on current and emerging policy problems. The Institution was founded on December 8, 1927, to merge the activities of the Institute for Government Research, founded in 1916, the Institute of Economics, founded in 1922, and the Robert Brookings Graduate School of Economics and Government, founded in 1924.

The Institution maintains a position of neutrality on issues of public policy. Interpretations or conclusions in Brookings publications should be understood to be solely those of the authors.

Copyright © 1997 by

THE BROOKINGS INSTITUTION

1775 Massachusetts Avenue, N.W., Washington, D.C. 20036

Library of Congress Cataloging-in-Publication Data

Fenno, Richard F., 1926—
    Learning to Govern: An Institutional View of the
  104th Congress / Richard F. Fenno Jr.
      p. cm.
    Includes bibliographical references (p.) and index.
    ISBN 0-8157-2785-2 (pbk.:alk. paper)
    1. United States. Congress. House.   2. United
  States—Politics and government—1993—   I. Title.
  JK1319.F45   1997
  328.73'072—dc21   97-21141
                                         CIP

9 8 7 6 5 4 3 2 1

The paper used in this publication meets the minimum requirements of the American National Standard for Information Sciences—Permanence of Paper for Printed Library Materials, ANSI Z39.48-1984

Typeset in Palatino

Composition by Harlowe Typography, Inc.
Cottage City, Maryland

Printed by Kirby Lithographic Co.
Arlington, Virginia

Foreword

THE 1994 ELECTIONS produced one of the most dramatic results in contemporary American political history—a Republican tide powerful enough to end the unprecedented forty-year Democratic reign in the House of Representatives. Quite apart from the partisan reactions, most serious students of Congress were heartened by the potential benefits of this alteration in party control for the functioning of American democracy. Giving members of both parties experience in and responsibility for governing ought to encourage more constructive behavior within the House and improve the climate of opinion outside.

This volume by Richard F. Fenno Jr., Distinguished University Professor and Kenan Professor of Political Science at the University of Rochester, examines the effects on governance of this sudden reversal of one-party dominance in the House of Representatives. Fenno argues that the total absence of first-hand political experience by the new Republican majority led to serious mistakes in interpreting their electoral victory and in governing the country, which ultimately frustrated their legislative agenda and paved the way for the rehabilitation and re-election of Bill Clinton. And instead of the hoped for civic renewal, the 104th Congress produced more partisan confrontation inside the institution and more public distrust of Congress outside. The implications of Fenno's institutional analysis are clear: more frequent alteration in party control of the legislature is essential for the health and vitality of our democratic institutions.

The initial version of this essay was presented as the Edward Douglas White Lectures on Citizenship at Louisiana State University in April 1997. The author wishes to thank the members of the LSU Department of Political Science for their invitation, good advice, and hospitality. He especially wishes to thank Cecil Eubanks, and also Jim Garand, Wayne Parent, and Jim Stoner. He also thanks Tom Mann and Sarah Binder at Brookings for their various forms of encouragement and good ideas. James Schneider edited the manuscript, Sally Martin proofread the pages, and Julia Petrakis compiled the index.

The views expressed in this book are those of the author and should not be ascribed to those acknowledged above or to the trustees, officers, or staff members of the Brookings Institution.

Michael H. Armacost
President

August 1997
Washington, D.C.

Contents

ONE

———————————————

Forty Years

I AM a Congress watcher. And for any Congress watcher
the 104th Congress surely stands out as one of the most
fascinating of recent times. For me the fascination grows
out of one simple historical fact: the 104th was the first
Congress in forty years in which the Republican party
controlled the House of Representatives. Every account
of the 104th Congress mentions it. But none of them
makes anything of it. I want to tell a story that *does* make
something out of it.

Certainly, there is nothing in our history to match this
forty-year stretch—from 1955 to 1995—without an alternation in party control of the House. In the one hundred
years from 1855 to 1955, the longest previous span of
one-party dominance was sixteen years. The Republicans did it twice, from 1859 to 1875 and from 1895 to 1911,
and the Democrats did it once, from 1931 to 1947. Indeed,
forty years is an extraordinarily long time for one-party
control of any democratically elected national legislature.
During the same four decades that one party controlled

our House of Representatives, for example, majority-party control of the British House of Commons changed hands four times, and the least victorious party ran the institution for nearly one-quarter of the period.

Forty years of unchanging partisan dominance may be very idiosyncratic. But it is enough of a phenomenon to have had some effect on the Congress that finally broke the mold, the 104th. Certainly, it was enough of a phenomenon to have had an effect on political scientists. For all those years we Congress watchers simply assumed that politics in the House of Representatives meant Democratic politics. We wrote extensively about the House Democrats, and we became the victims of our Democratic diet. We were quite unprepared to answer the question posed for us by the events of 1994—the question of long-term one-party dominance and the effects of its sudden reversal.

For students of Congress the question is "What effect did twenty consecutive Democratic Congresses have on the activity of the first Republican Congress that followed?"

For me the question has been stimulated by the counterfactual hunch that had we experienced even some minimal alternation in party control during the forty preceding years, the politics of the 104th Congress would have been different from what it was. My hunch is that those years of one-party control of the House helped produce some serious consequences, among which were the confrontational leadership behavior of Newt Gingrich, the deterioration in cross-party civility in the House, the Republican-led movement for term limits, and the accelerated decline of public confidence in Congress as an institution. Whatever the validity of these hunches, they have reenforced my idea that forty years without a change of party control had a major impact on the activities of the House of Representatives in the 104th

Congress. And the House, let us not forget, is the institutional centerpiece of our system of representative democracy.

The argument I want to make is that forty consecutive years as the minority party in the House left the Republicans, as of November 1994, totally without first-hand political experience of two essential sorts: first, experience in *interpreting* electoral victory and, second, experience in *governing* the country. In both respects, the relevant experience had been available only to the Democratic majority. The Republicans' lack of relevant experience, together with their accumulated frustrations, I shall argue, led the new majority to make serious mistakes, first of interpretation and then of governance. Because of their inexperience and their mistakes, the House Republicans missed their golden governing opportunity and made possible the rehabilitation, resurgence, and reelection of Bill Clinton.

This argument is deliberately more developmental and more institutional than the accounts produced by observers who were close to the day-to-day action in Washington and who focused their analysis on the three leading players—Newt Gingrich, Bob Dole, and Bill Clinton. Elizabeth Drew, author of *Showdown*, a book about the first fifteen months of the 104th Congress, concluded her analysis this way:

> A great deal—no less than the role of the federal government—was at stake last year and is again this year. The histories of these battles cannot be understood in abstraction from the nature, and the interplay among, the three major *personalities* who commanded them.[1]

Similarly, Michael Weisskopf and David Maraniss, authors of *"Tell Newt to Shut Up!,"* their book about the 104th, concluded,

This winter's historic struggle over the role of government has turned on a number of inter-twined factors: the clear clash of ideologies, the 1996 presidential campaign, the battle of political message. But in the midst of those larger forces were three men . . . whose goals and *personalities* played *the determining role* in shaping events.[2]

My story of the House of Representatives in the 104th Congress is perfectly compatible with accounts that center on personalities. And I shall rely heavily on such on-the-scene reports.[3] But my perspective is more institutional, more long term, and more generalizable than that of the journalists on the beat. Or so, as a practicing political scientist, I should like to think.

TWO

Electoral Interpretation and the Majority-Minority Relationship

THE PERIOD following an election is a critical time for every victorious political party. It is the time during which the winners decide for themselves what their victory meant and how it will shape their future activity. It is for them to interpret the election results; and it is their electoral interpretation that becomes the essential link between the business of campaigning and the business of governing. Everything that follows in the new Congress will be affected by the postelection interpretation of the winners. Political scientists will, of course, decide after many years and many Ph.D. dissertations what the voters' message *really* was. But the winning party cannot wait. It must choose its own working approximation early and will soon face the consequences.

The Republicans of 1994 had never faced this interpretive problem before. For twenty consecutive elections they had faced a very different problem: interpreting their defeat. And their interpretation had usually focused inward to a rash of blaming and bloodletting and to the cannibalizing of their leadership. This time, by contrast, their 1994 electoral interpretation would be their guide to governing the country. And this time their electoral interpretation was faulty. It set them off on the wrong course and was most unhelpful to them over the crucial year and a half that followed.

They chose to interpret their victory as an electoral mandate to undertake wholesale change, a mandate for what they called a Republican revolution. The election, they decided, had ratified their call for a *more responsive* government, by way of such constitutional changes as term limits, a balanced budget amendment, and a line-item veto, and their call for a *smaller* government, by way of legislative reductions in spending for a huge array of government programs.

So long as they described their mandate in the general language of change to a smaller, more responsive government and with an open-ended timetable, they retained some necessary flexibility in implementation. But the Republicans also decided in very concrete terms that the electorate had given its approval to their campaign document, the Contract with America. The document contained a lengthy list of policy proposals and a one-hundred-day timetable for completing House action on all of them. This more detailed electoral interpretation held that the public had voted support for a fairly specific program and for quick action to get it all under way. This refined reading of the election returns had two problems. There was scant evidence to support it. And, more important, it did not serve the party's long-term interest.

In the aftermath of the 1994 election, all available evidence told us that the election had been more a repudiation of the Democrats than an endorsement of the Republicans. Every incumbent House member, senator, and governor who lost was a Democrat. Every poll, plus the larger-than-normal midterm loss of Democratic seats, suggested an unusual degree of dissatisfaction with the Democratic president. Besides which, a large majority of voters had never heard of the Contract with America.

The voters had thrown out the Democrats and given the Republicans the opportunity to govern. But they had put the Republicans very much on trial and on a very short leash. Given their total lack of experience with Republican House majorities, the voters could hardly have done anything more than that. An accurate reading of the election results, therefore, would have been more provisional and more modest than the revolutionary ten-point-mandate interpretation the Republicans adopted.

The accuracy of an electoral interpretation may not, however, be the only measure of its usefulness to a victorious party. Something we might call strategic wisdom matters, too. If the victors adopt an empirically unsupportable electoral interpretation but can still make it work for them strategically—that is, if they can use it to help them achieve their most important goals—accuracy may not matter. Ronald Reagan's interpretation of a mandate in 1980 would be a case in point. In strategy as well as accuracy, however, the Republican postelection interpretation of 1994 was faulty.

If, as I think was the case, the party's most important long-run goal was to bring about a *unified Republican government*, the Republicans should have interpreted the election as an invitation to take some carefully selected first steps toward the accomplishment of that goal.

Since 1980 the Republican-conservative movement had held an intellectual advantage in the national policy debate over the performance of big government; and it had capitalized on that intellectual advantage to capture, for varying lengths of time, both the presidency and the Senate. But never the House. Viewed strategically, therefore, the Republicans' 1994 capture of the House was a long-awaited and necessary step toward the eventual achievement of a unified conservative government of the sort that Margaret Thatcher enjoyed for twelve years in Great Britain. But the 1994 election hardly signaled the completion of that journey. In which case the overriding task of the Republican 104th Congress was to keep building toward the capture of the 105th Congress and, most important, the presidency in 1996. To contemplate, much less proclaim, a revolution without having captured the presidency as well was pure fantasy.

An electoral interpretation that emphasized the incremental and instrumental nature of their governing opportunity would have constrained them to be cautious and selective in setting their legislative agenda. In the longer run what they most needed to accomplish was to retain their control over the terms of the national policy debate while also convincing an uncertain electorate that the country would function safely and smoothly in their hands. There was, in short, a huge difference between passing the Contract through the House in one hundred days and governing the country. A more modest, more provisional electoral interpretation would have encouraged the new majority to appreciate that difference and to subordinate the Contract to governing.

It is perfectly understandable, however, why the Republicans did not see the difference and why they chose the Contract-centered electoral interpretation they did. For one thing, they had never before had to interpret an election victory, and the absence of relevant past decisions created uncertainty. For another thing, forty years out of power had left them with a short fuse and a short time horizon. They had built up a massive backlog of frustration and energy. They had waited long enough. Understandably, patience and accommodation were not uppermost in their minds. They were anxious to seize the day and press their case as it was expressed in the Contract. Their inexperience plus their impatience blinded them to the government-wide stakes and to the long-run governing opportunities that had flowed from their electoral victory.

WHICH BRINGS US to the majority-minority relationship in the House. What does the relationship mean? What is it like to be in the minority in the House? Political scientists who study the two parties inside the legislature have found a great deal of structure and predictability in the majority-minority relationship. Based on the rules and practices of the House, certain recognizable and stable patterns of expectation, strategy, and behavior have developed. And they, as a bundle, define the relationship. Forty years of one-party rule in the House produced a recognizable, institutionally supported Democratic-Republican relationship. An equilibrium had been established, one unfavorable to the Republicans, but stable nonetheless. During four decades House Democrats learned only how to be a majority party, and House Republicans learned only how to be a minority party.

The two crucial structural features of the majority-minority relationship are first that *the majority party organizes* and runs the House and second that *the minority party adapts* to the governing majority. When the outgoing Democratic majority leader, Dick Gephardt, handed the gavel to the incoming Speaker, Newt Gingrich, on opening day January 1995, he said, "I hereby end 40 years of Democratic rule of this House."[1] *Rule* was the correct word. All our research tells us that the majority-party Democrats had long dominated the House floor and the House committees.

With respect to majority-party control of the House floor, consider these observations from Barbara Sinclair's authoritative studies of Democratic rule. "Consultation between the minority-majority parties on scheduling is rare in the House."[2] "The majority party leadership will structure [floor] rules so as to advantage the outcome its party members favor rather than that favored by the opposition party." "On major legislation meaningful participation in shaping the legislation and amassing support takes place . . . in the majority party." [3]

The majority party also controls committee activity— selecting leaders, shaping jurisdictions, assigning bills, setting committee size and majority-minority membership ratios, allocating staff resources, and establishing internal procedures. In a book that describes the majority party as "a legislative cartel," Gary Cox and Matt McCubbins conclude that "the legislative process in general—and *the committee system in particular*—is stacked in favor of majority party interests."[4] For forty years, whenever the House worked to reform its committee system, reforms were enacted by the majority party for the majority party, as repeated partisan struggles over minority staff resources and proxy voting attest.[5]

In short, the Republicans had little doubt about who organized and ran the House for forty years and who did not. A former member of the minority leadership compared his legislative influence with that of a majority party leader.

> As a Democrat, [he] set agendas; as a Republican, I reacted to them. As a Democrat, [he] helped to set the terms for debate, deciding what, if any, amendments would be considered when legislation reached the House floor; as a Republican, I pleaded with the Rules Committee for a chance to offer alternatives. As Democrats, [he] and his party's committee chairmen decided who

would be allowed to testify before congressional
committees and on what bills; as a Republican,
I had to fight to get conservative views heard.

And he concluded, "Congress belonged to the Democrats and they acted like it."[6]

More than that, the Democrats acted as if Congress
would belong to them for as far into the future as anyone
could see. And indeed, that was the commonly held
expectation throughout the period—that there was no
alternation in power in sight. Political science studies of
incumbency advantages, retirement ratios, and the career ambitions and strategic behavior of politicians all
pointed to continued Democratic hegemony.[7] National
surveys repeatedly showed that a majority of voters preferred Democrats to Republicans when voting for Congress.[8] And twenty consecutive election defeats kept rat-
ifying these assumptions.

Accordingly, students of Republican party politics became increasingly pessimistic about the chances of a
takeover. In his studies during the 1960s and 1970s
Charles Jones found that many Republicans were adopt-
ing a minority mentality, "accepting minority status as a
fact of life and accommodating themselves to their fate."[9]
And he maintained that their chances of becoming a
majority "do not appear very bright."[10] In their 1994
book, *Congress' Permanent Minority?*, William Connelly
and John Pitney concluded that "as of the early 1990's,
serious thoughts of a GOP Speakership are premature."[11]
Many safe and talented minority-party members accepted this growing judgment and, despairing of their
chances for attaining majority status, left the House.[12]

The widely shared expectation of continued Democratic party control affected the structure of incentives
inside the chamber. The idea here is that when both

parties expect to alternate in power, the party temporarily in the majority has an incentive to consult, cooperate with, and compromise with the party temporarily in the minority. A majority that expects one day to be in the minority is most likely to temper majority rule with a prudent respect for minority opinion. Under these circumstances, a sense of reciprocity develops between the two parties. But, goes the argument, when the majority party has not experienced minority status for decades and does not expect to be in the minority any day soon, the incentive for taking the minority into account is substantially reduced and a sense of reciprocity or comity is less likely to develop and persist. And that is what happened during forty years without any partisan alternation in power.

We can sense Democratic arrogance in such comments as these: from the majority leader, "Republicans are just going to have to get it through their heads that they are not going to write legislation."[13] From the majority whip, "What difference does it make what the Republicans think?"[14] From the Rules Committee chairman, "Hey, we've got the votes. Let's vote. Screw you."[15] From a top Education Committee staffer, "We rolled the Republicans every time. We had no fairness. We just screwed them."[16]

Webster's defines *frustration* as "a rendering vain or ineffectual all efforts however feeble or vigorous." And we can sense minority-party frustration in such comments as these: from the chairman of the Republican Policy Committee,

> [The Speaker] will do anything he can to win at any price, including ignoring the rules, bending the rules, writing rules, denying the House to work its will. It brings disrespect to the House itself. There's no sense of comity left. Why should you, if you are a Republican and given the way

Republicans are treated, think of a Democrat as a colleague? They aren't colleagues.[17]

Or from the minority leader,

Thirty-five years of uninterrupted power can act like a corrosive acid on the restraints of civility and comity. Those who have been kings of the hill for so long, may forget that majority status is not a divine right–and that minority status is not a permanent condition.[18]

Forty years of one-party rule—past, present, and projected—fostered a pattern of arrogance on one side and frustration on the other side of the majority-minority relationship in the House.

IF, AS I HAVE SAID, the first feature of the majority-minority relationship is that the majority governs, the second feature is that the minority adapts. As William Connelly and John Pitney put it, "while majority party members must debate how to govern the country, minority members must debate how to cope with their lowly place in the House."[19] From 1955 to 1995 the Republicans carried on an internal debate about the appropriate strategy of adaptation to the majority.

On one side were the *institutional partisans* who advocated accommodation and cooperation with the majority, who worked within the existing rules of the House to get whatever they could by way of bipartisan or cross-partisan policy adjustment. On the other side were the *confrontational partisans* who advocated aggressive in-your-face treatment of the majority, who cared little about legislative responsibility, and whose only goal was to drive the Democrats from power. As one of the party's future leaders said in 1993, "We're having a struggle right now within the Republican party . . . [between] those who think they're here to govern and those who think they're here to take over a majority. I am not among those here to govern. I am here to take over a majority from the Democrats."[20] In the beginning the institutional partisans, working in cross-party coalition with defecting conservative Democrats, won some legislative battles, and they prevailed inside the party. But the forty-year trend in the adaptation debate moved gradually with each influx of Republican newcomers away from a preferred strategy of institutional partisanship and toward a preferred strategy of confrontational partisanship.

The central theme among political scientists studying recent Congresses has been the steady increase in partisanship inside the House, "the resurgence of partisanship" in David Rohde's words.[21] If we study this resurgence from the majority party's perspective, the increase in partisanship is explained by a gradually more cohesive, more ideologically homogeneous, better organized, and more decisively led Democratic party. Those conditions influenced Republican partisanship, too, as conservative southern Democrats joined the Republican ranks. But if we write the forty-year story from the minority party's perspective, the increase in partisanship must also be explained in terms of the gradual change in Republican adaptation strategy as institutional partisans were replaced by confrontational partisans. The shift in the internal balance was finally completed when the leader of the confrontational partisans was elected as both the leader of his party and Speaker of the House.[22]

Which brings us to the one personality we cannot avoid: Newt Gingrich. For he was the architect, the leader, the articulator, and the symbol of the minority party's confrontational adaptation strategy in coping with the majority. In my story his ideas and his activities are *not* personality matters.[23] They are institutional matters. From the time he came to Congress in 1978 he thought about the House in institutional terms, that is, in terms of the majority party–minority party relationship. His overriding goal was to make the Republicans the majority party in the House. His instrumental goal was to change the party's adaptation strategy from accommodation to confrontation.

Six months into his House career he began criticizing his party's strategy of accommodation. "For a great part of its minority life," he said, "the Republican party has allowed itself to become coopted as an arm of the government. Too often, it has allowed itself to be cajoled into providing the necessary votes for the majority party to win."[24] "When I first came here," he later recalled, "the majority of the Republican caucus preferred passively accepting Democratic dominance and fighting them within a framework which Democrats and the establishment created."[25] "Democrats would go on the floor," he said, "to kick Republicans and show their contempt. The ranking Republicans would say how grateful they were to work with the chairman, when he had 70 staff people and the Republicans had three. It was the whole psychology of master and servant."[26] "I am interested," he said, "in breaking up the Democratic monopoly of power . . . the current one-sided rigging of the Rules Committee, the current rigging of the rules, the current liberal domination of scheduling and the current one-sided stamping on behalf of the Democrats."[27] And he vowed, "I will do almost anything to win a Republican majority in Congress."[28] From 1978 to 1994 he fought that battle. And its rationale was more institutional than personal.

He battled first by working to undermine two successive minority leaders, because he deemed them insufficiently confrontational. He and his soul mates pressured John Rhodes and then Bob Michel to be more aggressive in fighting Democrats than they wanted to be.[29] And that pressure contributed mightily both to the premature resignation of Rhodes and the premature retirement of Michel from their position as minority leader.[30]

Second, he battled by leading a sweeping attack on House Democrats. He attacked and humiliated Speaker Tip O'Neill for overstepping his bounds as presiding officer of the House.[31] He attacked Speaker Jim Wright for using his public position to enrich himself; and, in his greatest triumph, drove Wright from the House. "I am engaged in a long-term struggle," he explained. "The House is sick and Wright is the symbol."[32]

Third, he battled by attacking the House as an institution. When criticized for his personal attacks on Democratic leaders, he replied that his target was the institution itself. "This is about systemic, institutional corruption, not personality," he declared.[33] And he charged that "the Democrats have run the House for 30 years. They've gotten sloppy. The House is a corrupt institution in the Lord Acton sense."[34] By which he meant that "Power corrupts and absolute power corrupts absolutely."

In November 1994 the pursuit of this confrontational strategy produced the Republican majority he had so single-mindedly sought. It was an incredible success story. But success carried with it some serious costs as the new majority took up its governing tasks.

First, by attacking a generation of his own party's institutional partisans, he was attacking, in effect, the established interparty relationships that had given definition and stability to the House as an institution for four decades. More than that, he seemed to be ruling out accommodation as an acceptable mode of cross-party behavior. If so, he left very unclear what new kind of majority-minority equilibrium he intended to put in its place. He said vaguely that he wanted to bring about "a big, long-term cultural change" from a "collegial" institution to a "professional" one.[35] If what he wanted was less collegiality in the 104th Congress, he surely got it. "In all my years in Congress," said one twenty-four-year House Democrat in 1996, "I have never seen such bitter feelings between the minority and the majority."[36] The Republicans, he said later, "don't know how to run the place."[37]

Second, the scope and severity of Gingrich's partisan attacks earned him personally an implacable legacy of ill will from a large number of Democrats. In 1991 he admitted to being "the most hated man on Capitol Hill."[38] And as one of his soul mates in the Conservative Opportunity Society said, "it is not good or useful to be hated in this institution."[39] When asked to explain the "polarized and embittered" House in 1995, respected Republican veteran Henry Hyde cited "the absolutely pathological hatred of Newt Gingrich" by the Democrats.[40] Their persistent payback harassment of Speaker Gingrich continues to this day to inhibit cross-party cooperation.

Finally, by couching his attacks in the language of institutional corruption and the personal abuse of power, Gingrich deliberately manipulated and made worse an existing public cynicism and lack of confidence in the nation's most important representative institution. In attacking majority party arrogance, he was right on target. But it was impossible to hear or to read his yearly litany of indictments and to come away thinking well of the Congress as an institution. In working to take control of the House, he had also undermined and weakened it in the public eye.

Newt Gingrich and his confrontational style, I believe, were the predictable results of forty years in the minority. If it had not been him it would have been another confrontational partisan very much like him. Had there been an occasional alternation in power, and had the Republicans of the 104th Congress been able to know and to reap the rewards and responsibilities of running the institution earlier, they would, I think, have settled on a more accommodationist leadership style. The act of trading places occasionally would necessarily have introduced constraints on their partisanship. Alternation would also have produced a strong incentive to protect the existing institutional framework, placing greater emphasis on cross-party comity and reciprocity. The explanation for Newt Gingrich's rise to party leadership and for his subsequent leadership performance depends heavily on the extraordinary length of time his party had had to endure the deprivations and frustrations of an out-party minority.[41]

THREE

Governing: The Contract, the Freshmen, the Speaker

WHAT ABOUT the governing performance of the 104th Congress? The good news was that the Republican party had been given a once-in-a-lifetime opportunity. The bad news was that the Republican party had been given a once-in-a-lifetime opportunity. It was forty years since they had been in a position to govern. They were, arguably, the least experienced House majority in one hundred years. And it showed.

The party's new leader produced a torrent of rhetoric about governing. "This is a genuine revolution," said Gingrich. "We're going to rethink every element of the federal government. We're going to close down several federal departments."[1] But he had no idea how to do any of it. He was, after all, just a smart, articulate, visionary college professor. Governing was going to be a totally experimental adventure for him.

Again, there is nothing surprising about this state of affairs. The governing expertise the Republicans lacked was precisely the kind that can only be acquired through trial and error by those who have held power. The governing expertise of which I speak is not subject matter expertise, which minority members can acquire in their committees. It is expertise about the business of legislating. That business involves a practical grasp of lawmaking as a lengthy, incremental, multilevel, coalition-building process. And it involves a seasoned strategic sense in matters such as establishing priorities, negotiating outcomes across the separated institutions of government, and calculating feasibilities, trade-offs, and timing at every decisionmaking juncture. In short, successful governing takes a lot of practice, and the Republicans hadn't had any.

When the victorious Republicans huddled after the election—under the influence of their we-won-it-and-we-got-a-sweeping-mandate interpretation of the election results—they decided to take the document they had crafted for *electioneering* purposes, the Contract with America, and adopt it wholesale as their *legislative* agenda. The decision had the virtue of giving instant focus, organization, and work to a new, inexperienced, and impatient majority. But its conception of the governing process was every bit as faulty as the faulty electoral interpretation on which it rested.

First, because it had been packaged with the help of polls and focus groups for electoral purposes, the Contract lacked any sense for legislative priorities. It was a laundry list of ten vote-getting proposals, each placed on the same footing as every other by the promise that all would be brought to a vote in the House within one hundred days. Yet they were a very mixed bag. Some were broadly institutional, even constitutional, in their content and impact; others were more narrowly programmatic. They commanded varying patterns of support inside the party. Some drew support from the Democrats;

others served to mobilize the minority party in opposition. Their future prospects were, therefore, very uneven.

By prescribing an equality of effort and an identical time line for all items, the Republicans substituted inflexibility for subtlety. They deprived themselves of a chance to think about their legislative agenda in terms of trade-offs, or to make distinctions between what they would *like* to get and what they *had* to get. Participants in the legislative process typically have to settle for less than they might want. It is very important to know when to declare victory, when to take something for now and return for more later. The animating spirit of the one hundred days was, in the words of Policy Chairman Christopher Cox, that "revolutions have a very short half life. If you don't ask for it, you don't get it."[2] That spirit was inadequate preparation for life in the legislative lane. Indeed, when they discovered, late in the day, that the Contract left many priorities untouched, they started piling lots of normal legislation directly onto their appropriations bills, a hasty improvisation that misused the appropriations process, bogged down the flow of money bills, opened up jurisdictional battles inside the party, and brought embarrassing defeats on the House floor.[3]

In the second place the Contract conveyed no sense of a long-run strategy for actually enacting any of its proposals into law. It focused only on action inside the House. It took no account of the broader legislative context that lay beyond, a context of separated institutions, sharing responsibility and power. It took no cognizance of the Senate with its distinctive procedures and its different ideological makeup, nor did it comprehend the president with his veto power and his bully pulpit. This neglect of the larger context helped blind House Republicans to certain structural limitations on their power, for example, their very slim working majority of fourteen votes, a majority that would become vulnerable under external pressure and was not even close to being veto proof.

To be sure, the party did bring all ten Contract items to a vote in the House and they did pass nine of them there. They displayed an extraordinary diligence and discipline in doing so. When it was over, however, they talked and acted as if they had mastered the legislative process. Not only had they not understood the difference between passing the Contract and governing the country, but what was worse, they had mistaken one for the other. They took the view that they had passed the crucial performance test and were now ready for public judgment. "We did what we said we would do," they said. And they tirelessly repeated their slogan, "promises made, promises kept." It conveyed a far broader sense of accomplishment than was warranted.

Their performance on the Contract had, in fact, been a short-run, narrowly focused, inward-looking legislative performance. It had been at best a preliminary test of their governing ability at the beginning of a more complicated and longer-lasting legislative effort.

IT IS NOT possible to understand the interpretive and the governing failures of the new majority party in the 104th Congress without paying attention to *the freshman class* that made the majority possible. The seventy-three newcomers are important to this analysis for at least two reasons. First, they enjoyed an unusually large potential for intraparty influence. Second, if inexperience was a problem for the new majority, the freshman class would most likely exemplify the problem.

When political scientists estimate the influence potential of legislative parties or party groupings, we pay special attention to their size and to their cohesion on policy matters. In both respects the freshman Republicans had a great potential for influence. They were the second largest group of newcomers in either party since World War II, and they made up one-third of their party's majority. They wore buttons that said, "Majority Maker," and they relished the prospect of their pivotal decision-making power inside the Republican caucus. They were not only an unusually large group, they were an unusually cohesive group. As some long-time observers noted, "They arrived on Capitol Hill with a sense of common purpose that has rarely been seen in any incoming class of congressmen."[4] And they "developed an unusually strong sense of class cohesion."[5] They shared a short-run commitment to the Contract with America; and they shared a long-run determination to transform their conservative policy preferences into a new pattern of government. Conservative commentators exulted in their presence. "When and if the leadership blinks, the freshman class will go on point," predicted Kate O'Bierne of the Heritage Foundation."[6]

Any large turnover in House membership is likely to be a source of new ideas, and the 1994 turnover certainly qualified as large. Even more relevant to their potential for policy influence was that sixty-five of the seventy-three newcomers—90 percent of them—came from constituencies that had been represented by Democrats in the 103d Congress. Students of the linkage between elections and public policy have found that these switched-seat newcomers, fresh from a victory over the opposing party, are the most potent carriers of new policy ideas. Historically, when there is an extra large influx of switched-seat newcomers into the majority party in Congress, major policy changes follow.[7] Sixty-five switched-seat Republican freshmen certainly qualified as an extra large influx. And they certainly had a missionary spirit when it came to changes in policy direction. As they frequently explained their zeal for change, "That's what I came here for."[8]

There were, of course, plenty of differences within the group. And we should not forget that. But because of their unusual potential for influence, they quickly came to be viewed by others as a collectivity. The media paid them an inordinate amount of attention. Headlines read: "A Class of New Warriors," "The GOP's Young Turks," "73 Mr. Smiths, of the GOP, Go To Washington," "The Transformers," "Freshmen: New Powerful Voice."[9] All seventy-three were lumped together and described variously as the "shock troops," "revolutionaries," "ideological firebrands," "giant killers," "red guards" of the new majority, and as "the 800 pound gorilla of Washington politics."[10]

They were not at all bashful about accepting these descriptions, since they, too, thought of themselves as a collective force. "[I am] not meaningful," said one member, "but the word 'freshman' is meaningful."[11] Accordingly, they spoke of themselves regularly as the freshman class. Listen to some of their self-characterizations, each from a different member.

> The freshman class is the best representation of an absolute commitment to change.[12]

> The difference between the freshmen and the people who have been here for a while is that we're closer to the people. We're more responsive to what they want to do.[13]

> The freshman class is prepared to go to the wall for what we believe in.[14]

This freshman class has shown that we have
the courage to stand up to this institution, even to
our own leadership.[15]

We're solid as a rock. There's no quit in this
freshman class. We're going to keep pushing.[16]

Self-consciously and self-confidently they thought of
themselves as a force to be reckoned with in the 104th
Congress. As one freshman said to me, "The freshman
class is a real thing."

As a group, therefore, the freshmen were long on size
and cohesion. They were also long on conviction and
confidence. But they were short on another major attri-
bute of legislative influence—experience. Fewer than
half (thirty-five) had previous electoral experience. Of
that group, only seventeen had any experience in a state
legislature; and of that group, just seven had any experience as a member of the majority party in a state
legislature. All told, therefore, only seven of the seventy-
three Republican newcomers had any governing experience as a member of a legislative majority, which was, of
course, the situation that faced them in the 104th Congress. In an inexperienced majority party, they were the
least experienced of all.

As far as I can tell, however, they did not think their
lack of governing experience diminished their potential
for influence. Some even wore this deficiency as a badge
of distinction. "Our class symbol should be the bumble
bee," said one. "Aeronautical engineers say the bumble
bee can't fly because there's not enough wing size to
carry its weight. But the bumble bee flies because he
never studied aeronautical engineering."[17] Many of his
classmates shared that cavalier attitude toward political
experience.

They thought of themselves, instead, as citizen legislators, for whom it was precisely their nonpolitical experience that would be their most important contribution
to the business of governing. Because they were coming
from the nonpolitical, workaday world, they saw themselves as bringing the real life experiences of ordinary
people to bear on the work of an insulated Congress.
They associated extended governing experience with a
corrupting, self-aggrandizing careerism that produced
professional politicians who were out of touch with
everyday reality. Central to their self-image was a devotion to term limits. And that special Republican devotion,
I believe, was yet another product of forty years as the
minority party in the House.

As citizen legislators, many of them had put a limit
on their temporary assignment in Washington and had
promised to return in a forseeable future to the daily life
of the country from which they had come. They were
prepared to get their legislative experience on the job.
But because they had short-run career horizons, they
were not prepared to wait to get their experience before
they tried to make a difference. Their newcomers' enthu-
siasm, coupled with their short-run career horizons,
fueled an attitude of "let's get it all, and get it all now."

THE FIRST decisions on which the freshman class had the
chance to make a difference were those involving the
interpretation of their electoral victory. Because only
seven had ever been involved in this kind of decision
before, they had little independent judgment to offer.
Not surprisingly, they totally embraced the interpretation
of a sweeping mandate, the one that assumed voter approval of a Republican revolution. Because, as candidates, they had introduced themselves most recently *to*
the electorate and now, as House members, had come
most recently *from* the electorate, they were confident

that they understood the electoral mandate better than most. If they added anything independently to the interpretive process, therefore, it was a heightened sense of urgency about the party's mission and a desire for a quickened legislative pace. As one of them put it, "The freshman class is not a do-nothing class. This is a do-something-and-do-it-all-right-now freshman class."[18]

They quickly seized on the Contract with America as the authentic expression of their electoral mandate. Most had signed it; many were familiar with it from their campaigns. "The three most important issues for the freshman class," said one member, "are the Contract, the Contract, and the Contract."[19] Some wore their laminated copies around their necks. Others kept it with them always, in a coat pocket. Some called it "my Bible."[20] Even the few who had not signed the Contract gave it top priority. As one such member said, "I think the Contract, for the vast majority of the freshmen, is their Bible. We've got to sell it and pass it before we do anything else."[21] Although all of them acknowledged Newt Gingrich as their leader, they were prepared to hold his feet to the fire when the Contract was involved. As their class president said, "We intend to keep the pressure on the leadership not to deviate from the Contract."[22]

The freshmen became the proprietary guardians of the Contract. As each important item passed, they basked in media attention. Wearing buttons that read "Keeping Promises," and amid signs proclaiming "Promises Made, Promises Kept," they celebrated ceremoniously by putting check marks in the appropriate boxes on wall-sized charts and in their personal copies. When it was completed, they held a grand celebratory reprise on the Capitol steps.

Several times during the 104th Congress, I journeyed to the districts of two members of the freshman class.

My conversations with them can add some insight into the dynamics of the 104th, first on interpreting the election, later on governing the country. They were in no sense representative of the class. From different parts of the country, from different backgrounds, and with differing ambitions, they were nonetheless typical of the class in some essential respects. They were deep-dyed conservatives, enthusiastic reformers, committed citizen legislators, and 100 percent supporters of the Contract. Neither man ever seemed the least bit jaded or cynical about the politics they were engaged in. Neither one was a shrinking violet within the class.

Both men subscribed to the idea that their victory was an electoral mandate and that the Contract with America was of crucial importance. It may be indicative of the very strong hold the Contract had on the group that both men embraced it so wholeheartedly, even though it played virtually no part in either of their election campaigns. Both men campaigned almost exclusively against Bill Clinton.

One campaigned by attacking his 1994 opponent as "a Clinton clone." His TV ads "morphed" his opponent's face into Clinton's face. Yet he eagerly signed the Contract and fully embraced it afterward. His action was based, he said, on "the ethics of campaigning." When he signed the Contract, in his view he made a promise; and once elected he was committed to fulfill that promise. That is what the voters expected him to do: pass the Contract, come home, and campaign on that basis.

It was a lofty embrace. If politicians hoped to retain public trust, he believed, they must maintain this link between campaigning and governing. As he explained in 1995,

> George Bush's idea was that the two were separate, that you campaigned on a platform and then

governed without regard to it. That view bred cynicism. The new cohort of Republicans is saying, "hold us accountable." That puts us on the right path. And I can see a changed ethic in Washington.

For him, there was simply no other intellectual basis for an electoral intrepretation than the Contract and its promises. His 1996 reelection campaign headquarters was dominated by a huge sign, "Promises Made, Promises Kept." All of his 1996 campaign brochures and his TV ads carried the slogan, "He did what he said he would do," or "he kept his word." If this freshman ever saw any problems with the Contract, he never mentioned it. Indeed, toward the end of the 104th he began to advocate a second Contract.

When I first met the second freshman, shortly after the one hundred days, he volunteered,

> By far the biggest factor in my election was Bill Clinton. People here were against everything he did. . . . When I first heard about the Contract, I was reluctant [to sign]. I was not real enthusiastic. I was happy running against Bill Clinton. . . . [But] the Contract gave me an agenda to talk about . . . [it] nationalized the election. That was its biggest contribution.

If, therefore, the Contract had a nationalizing effect, what better vehicle to serve as their defining electoral mandate? His attitude after the election was, "If we're going to make the voters feel good about giving Republicans all these seats, the first thing we need to do is implement the Contract." Unlike his colleague, however, he did show signs of second-guessing his early electoral interpretation.

In April 1996 I had no sooner climbed into his car than he asked me, "What happened in 1994? Did we win or did they lose?" "I think they lost," I said. "So, did we blow it?" he asked. "Yes," I said. "I think you blew it." It was the right question. But the answer had come too late. Six months later, he returned to his party's crucial interpretative mistake.

> When the Republicans held their very first conference after the election, there was a question I was dying to ask. And I've been kicking myself in the butt ever since for not asking it. I wanted to ask, "Did we win or did they lose?" If you think we won, give me five things you think we ought to do. If you think they lost, give me five things you think they should do. You can't figure out where you want to go until you take an inventory of what it was that got you there. The other question I wanted to ask was, "If you were in their place, what would you do?" We acted like we won. We never asked ourselves what the Democrats would do.

Whether or not his reconstruction was accurate, he was coming to understand the costs of his party's inexperienced rush to electoral interpretation.

The passage in the House of all but one Contract item in one hundred days was, indeed, a remarkable achievement, one worth celebrating—but with one cheer, not three. It was, I have argued, a self-contained, narrowly focused, inward-looking, short-run achievement. Its highly acclaimed workload statistics—time in session, pages of debate, measures reported, number of roll calls—reflected the ability to organize majority party power inside the House. But that achievement rested on a mistaken electoral interpretation, and a mistaken understanding of the overall governing process in the American political system. To the extent, therefore, that the freshman class enshrined and enforced the Contract with America, and it surely did, their guardianship only made the inadequacies of that document worse. Their attachment to the Contract introduced a big dose of rigidity into the legislative process, helping to set the party on a governing path that would be difficult to change.

THE ORGANIZATION of majority-party power inside the House was one thing Newt Gingrich *had* been planning well in advance of the 1994 election. His goal was to further centralize power. And his plans focused on the increased subordination of committee power to the power of majority party leadership.[23] But the underlying institutional condition that made further party centralization possible was this: the party had been out of power for so many years. As his predecessor, Speaker Tom Foley, explained, "I don't think any Democratic Speaker would be in quite the same situation as Speaker Gingrich. . . . There have been no Republican committee chairmen for over 40 years. . . . So he's had a *blank slate* on which to write and that has given him a great deal of influence.[24]

Seizing this opportunity, the new Speaker abolished some committees and subcommittees, appointed the committee chairmen, extracted loyalty pledges from committee leaders, controlled committee staff, selected committee members, created and staffed ad hoc task forces to circumvent committees, established committee priorities and time lines, and monitored committee compliance. The end product was an American version of a prime minister in a system of party government and a legislative process with a lot less of the deliberative and incremental pacing that a committee-centered system can provide. Political scientists have produced a number of fascinating studies of the new Speaker's effort to centralize majority party power.[25]

He carried out these changes with the approval of the Republican caucus, but he did it with such efficient dispatch—in concert with a small advisory group—that there were few opportunities for dissent. Where the freshman class was concerned, of course, he had the advantage of forethought and experience. But in any case, the incoming group was strongly predisposed to follow his lead. Ideologically, they considered themselves his children and politically his beneficiaries. The conservatism they brought increased the homogenity of preferences within the party that analysts of "conditional party government" associate with an increased willingness to cede power to party leaders.[26]

To gain some perspective on the governing opportunities of the 1994 freshman class, it is helpful to compare it with the 1974 class of freshman Democrats, the seventy-five so-called Watergate babies. The two groups, the largest of the past half century, were equally big and equally self-conscious of themselves as a class. The Class of '74, too, had captured a very large number of seats from the other party: forty-nine of the seventy-five, or 65 percent. As switched-seat occupants they, like their 1994 cousins, were aggressive advocates of institutional and policy change. And in the end, both groups had a measurable impact on the governing activities of their respective partisan majorities. But the instructive difference between them was that the liberal freshman Democrats of 1974 were joining a long-standing, well-organized majority party that had been running the House for twenty years, whereas the conservative freshman Republicans of 1994 were joining a brand new majority party. One group was constrained by entrenched power; the other group was not.

Because their party was already enjoying power in the House, the 1974 freshman Democrats were prepared to govern within the constraints of established power relationships. The Speaker they had to deal with, Carl Albert, was strongly attached to the organizational status quo. He was, Ronald Peters has written, "closely tied to the committee system and the barons who ran it. . . . [He] and the freshman Democrats talked past each other as if they were speaking different dialects."[27] And Albert had a seventy-three-vote majority. The freshmen, therefore, were constrained to adopt an incremental reform strategy, one designed to free the ordinary member from the constraints of hierarchy and seniority, or as they put it, to give rank and file members "a piece of the action." Most visibly, they spearheaded the unprecedented unseating of three veteran committee chairmen. The 1974 freshman class became the essential catalyst in accelerating the gradual decentralization of decision structures and the gradual diffusion of member influence that came to characterize "the postreform Congress."[28]

The 1994 class, by contrast, faced few settled partisan routines and established party hierarchies. The Speaker they dealt with was openly and deeply in their debt. "When I see a freshman," said Newt Gingrich, "I see the majority. They had a huge influence. I wouldn't be Speaker if they weren't here."[29] The freshman Republicans, therefore, came to Capitol Hill with an expansive, almost open-ended, sense for the possibilities of change and for their own participatory opportunities. The diminution of committee power that the Democratic Speaker had resisted in 1974 the Republican Speaker engineered on his own in 1994. The freshmen accepted the view that if the Republicans were to change Washington, party power in the House would have to be centralized. They were a lot less concerned about getting a piece of the action than they were about facilitating the revolution. They accepted, therefore, a nonincremental reform strategy, precisely the opposite course from their 1974 counterparts. And in the beginning at least, they fully acquiesced in the largest concentration of majority-party power in a century.

The freshmen's willingness to support radical internal change was further buttressed by their strong anti-institutional preferences, as expressed in the Contract. Those sentiments, too, were different from those in the 1970s. Whether they actually campaigned on the Contract or not, the 1994 freshmen overwhelmingly campaigned in favor of its central institutional elements: term limits, the balanced budget amendment, and the line-item veto. Singly or in combination, these items represented an attack on the performance of Congress as a political institution.

In one sense this attack was nothing new. During research travels in the 1970s I found most incumbent House members "running *for* Congress by running *against* Congress."[30] But they did so in a retail fashion, as a backdrop for personal self-congratulation and with language customized by individual members to fit their individual constituencies. Their criticisms did not cumulate in a way that would generate new governing programs or strategies.

In 1994, however, the anti-institutional message of the freshman candidates was the same nearly everwhere in the country. It was a coordinated, wholesale, frontal attack on the institution, promising three major changes in the power of Congress within the American political system. That was something new. The 1974 Democratic freshmen—perhaps because their party was in power—campaigned without broadside attacks on Congress. In 1994 a large group of legislators came to power having made a broad institutional argument. Further, theirs was an argument that dovetailed nicely with the institutional argument that their leader had been making for sixteen years. Their platform had attacked to an unprecedented degree the power and prerogatives of the very institution through which they proposed to govern. At the very least the freshmen were without any strong attachment to existing organizational forms in the House.

The new Speaker faced the unusual task of organizing a new system of party government and at the same time absorbing seventy-three inexperienced newcomers into the governing party. Experience had taught him a lot about freshmen. Every two years for fourteen years he had welcomed, socialized, organized, and energized each incoming Republican class. They became the building blocks of his new confrontational majority. "My strategy," he said, "was always [that] you would capture 70 to 80% of the incoming freshmen every two years and at some point, you would have transformed the whole structure."[31] That is what finally happened in 1994.

He dealt with his final freshman building block generously. He gave them an unprecedented number of assignments—twenty-four—to the five blue-ribbon House committees.[32] He involved then in the unusually important work of the task forces that he used to bypass committees. He met with them in weekly luncheons; he talked with them constantly; and he kept their noses to the grindstone.[33] In this latter respect the Contract was a success, a huge success. For one hundred days it focused, harnessed, preempted, and preoccupied the time and energies of a very ideological, very impatient freshman class. Who knows how they might have busied themselves otherwise?

As the Speaker quickly learned, however, governing with the freshmen would be a dicey enterprise. With a slim fourteen-vote partisan margin, he needed all of them. A dozen or so recalcitrant freshmen (or any others) meant big trouble. They signalled as much early on when they fought him on the balanced budget amendment over a provision requiring a three-fifths vote to raise taxes.[34] Most of the time they were his allies. Freshman support for the leadership on roll call votes outpaced that of the rest of the Republicans.[35] Still, the relationship was one of mutual dependence. It required fairly constant monitoring and bargaining, especially on amendments. As he described it, "I am the leader of a broad coalition. I'm not a dictator. We have 73 freshmen. You don't get them marching in a line. You get them sort of saying, 'Maybe I'll be with you. Call back in an hour.'"[36] As freshman members described the relationship, "Some of the time Gingrich uses us because he agrees with us. And some of the time he doesn't have a choice."[37] Or, "On some issues, we run him and on other issues, he runs us."[38] Of all the groups he had to deal with in the majority, the freshmen were the biggest and most consequential. The complexity and the uncertainty of their bargaining relationship would become amply evident during the fateful conflict over the budget.

FOUR

The Budget Confrontation and Its Aftermath

AMONG the governing tests that lay beyond the House and beyond the one hundred days, the most consequential for House Republicans was the passage of their balanced budget. Passing the Contract was not synonymous with governing the country; but passing the balanced budget was. It contained, in dollars and cents language, the sum and substance of their smaller-government conservatism. It was a test that finally forced the House Republicans to contemplate the separation of powers and to cope with the conflicting budgetary views, interests, and strategies of other legislative players, especially the president of the United States.[1]

If my argument is correct, they were woefully ill equipped for that encounter. Both their early postelection assumption that the voters had called for a "push hard and get it all now" mission and their later post-Contract assumption that they knew how to work the legislative process ran contrary to the evidence. Both

37

assumptions reflected the inexperience, and the frustration, of a party that had not been in a position to govern in decades. And both had already led to ill-advised strategies. Nonetheless, in the mistaken belief that they commanded both public support for their revolution and the capacity to make the revolution happen, the Republicans decided to force the president to accept their budgetary blueprint in its entirety, even if it meant shutting down the federal government.

This posture, confident and militant, was the external manifestation of Newt Gingrich's career-long adaptation strategy of confrontational partisanship. And it reflected the same uncompromising spirit. On election night, Gingrich prefigured the coming institutional confrontation with the president. "If you are going to operate with his veto being the ultimate weapon . . . you have to find a trump to match his trump. And the right not to pass money bills is the only trump that is equally strong."[2]

Very early in constructing a balanced budget bill, he set a tone of inflexibility by formally binding his leadership group, by vote, to a seven-year timetable that would be "etched in stone."[3] When the government first closed for lack of money, he defined the moment in portentous terms. "If we cave," he said, "it'll be clear to this country that the best chance we've had in a generation to balance the budget will have failed—not postponed—failed."[4] He had no doubt that the president would cave and would accept the terms of the Republican balanced budget. He stipulated, in public, exactly what the president had to do to win Republican approval.[5] "I know the smell and rhythm of this city," he added, "and I am confident we are going to get it."[6] The public, he believed, stood behind their presumed electoral mandate. "They are counting on us keeping our word," he said, "because they actually believe we are different."[7]

When the President refused to sign a continuing resolution to keep money flowing to the departments and agencies because he would not accept a wholly extraneous and ineptly conceived rider affecting medicare, a large part of the government closed. Gingrich predicted, without any sense of consternation, that the shutdown could "easily last 90 days."[8] And, typically, he portrayed the budget dispute in all-or-nothing apocalyptic terms. "It will decide for a generation who we are. This is not a game of political chicken. . . . This is a serious, historic debate and a serious historic power struggle."[9] When public opinion registered on the shutdown, however, disapproval of Republican congressional behavior stood at a whopping 71 percent.[10]

Even so, after a brief reopening the Republicans, confident that "Clinton would do what he always had done, cave and cut a deal," once again shut off the money and shut down the government.[11] For three weeks, off and on, legislative-executive negotiations continued. Finally, under pressure from the Senate, from some Republican House members, and ultimately from the public, the Republicans backed down, abandoned their goal of a balanced budget, and negotiated with the president to fund the government. Gingrich admitted to the president's negotiator, Leon Panetta, "Our strategy has not worked. We thought we could break you. . . . We've got a failed strategy on our hands."[12]

Their unsuccessful budget confrontation with the president demonstrated beyond any doubt how little the new majority knew about the legislative process, about its inevitable incrementalism, trade-offs, compromises, negotiations, and public resonances. For one thing, budget politics is *always* incremental politics. It is never apocalypic politics. You can't possibly run a revolution through the budget process. But you can use budget increments to demonstrate that you have taken some steps to change the direction of government and the terms of public debate. You can then declare victory on that account and take an overall record of forward motion to the electorate.

With the slightest bit of strategic sense, the Republicans could have done this by declaring victory at several junctures during the budget negotiations. Indeed, numerous observers claimed victory on their behalf.[13] They pointed out the concessions made by the president, and they recorded the small but widespread reductions being made in discretionary expenditures. They credited the Republicans with a substantial "conservative correction," if not a revolution. When the president made obvious budgetary concessions, however, it was the White House that commanded the interpretative spin.[14] Despite their incremental victories, therefore, the Republicans lost the opportunity to control the public dialogue and take the offensive in claiming progress.

In the end, Republican pressure did cause the president to submit a balanced budget, make large reductions in medicare, set a seven-year timetable, and permit Crogressional Budget Office participation. And when the government reopened, the president offered a budget that had moved closer to the Republicans than anyone thought possible.[15] Even then, they could have achieved a balanced budget and maintained control of the the public debate by celebrating each of these presidential concessions as a small step toward the reduction of spending and the making of a conservative government. But, again, they declined to negotiate. To do so, Gingrich maintained, would be to have "sold out all the values we came to Washington to promote [for] one more phony Washington deal."[16] It was the last call for House Republicans. Having taken the wrong path in the beginning, they seemed to be determined to stay on it.

By contrast, Senate leader Bob Dole, who had experienced majority party power and leadership from 1981 to 1986, advocated just such a series of small steps and small claims. For him, legislation should always be considered work in progress. "You get something this year," he advised, "and you get more next year." And he insistently pressed his House counterparts with the question, "What's your end game?" But as the president's budget negotiator knew, Gingrich had given no thought to what, in the end, he might settle for or what he could deliver. As Leon Panetta said, "He came to the table not to negotiate, but to dictate the terms of surrender."[17]

From the beginning their electoral interpretation had pointed the Republicans toward a narrow, short-run view of governing. And because of that view, they were not positioned to settle for—and take credit for—incremental steps that would keep them in control of the public debate and keep them moving them toward a goal of a unified Republican government. What a party can effectively claim in governing is related to the expectations it sets, and the Republicans' electoral interpretation set expectations that effectively ruled out incrementalist and gradualist governing claims.

The Contract with America was particularly unhelpful as it affected the budgetary behavior of the freshman class. At the time of the budget confrontation their experience with the Contract was the only governing experience they had known. It left them, after one hundred days of success, with a heady but false sense of their power and a false sense of their accomplishment. They came to the budget conflict with an exaggerated idea of their capacity to shape outcomes, an unrealistic idea of how much they could win through a refusal to compromise, and an underdeveloped idea of what the business of governing looked like in the world beyond the House. Reflecting on their budgetary performance, a conservative senator commented, "I'd feel a lot more confident about the outcome of the revolution if I were convinced all of these guys had taken high school civics."[18]

The newcomers styled themselves "the conscience of the congressional Republicans," and as such they injected a dose of inflexibility into budget making.[19] Listen, for example, to three of the ringleaders describe their view of the impending conflict: "*We're* not going to give in. If there has to be a train wreck, there will be a train wreck."[20] "*We're* going to stand for principle. The consequences be damned." "Maybe not all 73, but 50 to 55 of us don't care if we're reelected if we fold on the balanced budget."[21] In legislative politics it is far easier to block than to build. And the freshmen were better at blocking than building majorities. It was they who insisted, to the end, on "Congressional Budget Office scoring" and the seven-year timetable.[22] Their posture crippled the Speaker in his negotiations and compounded the governing problems of the new majority.

At the climactic moment it was the intransigence of the freshman vanguard that forced the Speaker to admit to executive branch negotiators that he could not deliver on *any* agreement the two sides might reach.[23] And it was the same freshmen that forced him, in effect, to put his Speakership to a vote in the caucus before they agreed to his proposal to reopen the government. They turned against him the very same aggressiveness they had imbibed from him. In the end, the freshmen bore a heavy responsibility for the government shutdown and for the long-run repercussions that followed.

The two freshmen with whom I travelled were typically short on legislative experience. One had none and the other had served for two years in a state legislature in the minority party. Both were passionately dedicated to the passage of a balanced budget, and both expended special efforts in that cause. In their postmortem assessments they spoke from different perspectives. But both acknowledged learning the same basic lesson: governing the country requires that all relevant players must be taken seriously into account.

One of them recalled his efforts during budget negotiations.

> I remember being warned in August when Alice Rivlin sent around a memo saying, in essence, 'if you are going to shut the government down, you had better be ready to tell us what programs you want to sacrifice and which ones you want to save.' That told me that they meant serious business; and I suggested to our leadership that we should be ready with our priorities in case they put the question to us. They said that it wasn't necessary, that if the government was shut down, it would not be for long. . . . Several times I said that we should think of Clinton's budget position as the start of his reelection campaign and deal with it appropriately. The senior guys would say 'we hear you,' but they didn't take it seriously. They thought Clinton wanted a budget deal. They probably thought here was some freshman who hadn't had any experience. It was a disaster . . . the momentum of 1994 came to an end. . . . And worst of all, it left us without a plan for the summer.

Accurate or not, his reconstruction reflects his awareness of the separated and shared powers so basic to our system. When asked back home what he had learned after fifteen months in office, he replied, "We overstated what the freshmen could do, what with the Senate able to disagree with our ideas and the president able to knock them down. . . . I learned the limits of what the House could do by itself."

The second freshman was among the hard-liners. As
he recalled,

Our poll numbers were dropping, but I believed
they had slipped as far as they were going to go. I
was one of the fiery ones saying "no, no, don't
give in." The president had agreed that we would
each put a balanced budget on the table. We had
produced ours. He had not produced his. The is-
sue was keeping his word. I went on national tele-
vision twice and said that if anyone lied to me like
that in private business, I'd never have anything
to do with that person as long as I lived. Then
Dole put a continuing resolution through the Senate that provided for opening the government. I
lost a lot of respect for Bob Dole right there. When
it came to our conference, I was madder than I've
ever been in politics. I asked Newt, "Did you
know Dole was going to do this?" He said he did
and I said, "Why didn't you tell us?"

He had learned that the weak, pushover president he
had routed in the 1994 campaign context was a much
more formidable president in the institutional context.
"The president had smart advisors," he said. "They had
a budget all the time, but they held it back so long as our
numbers were dropping and we were getting the blame.
He played us like a fiddle. . . . We had no exit strategy.
We knew how to get started, but not how to stop." And
he concluded, "we had all been saying to ourselves, 'this
is so neat. Everything is going to work for us.' We forgot
to worry about how the other person was thinking or
what the other person might do."

Both newcomers were especially critical of their party's ineptness with the media during the budget confrontation. "We did a terrible job of marketing our position," said the hard-liner. "If we had sold our position

better, we could have hung on and won." And his colleague elaborated, "One area where we failed terribly was communications. If we keep the House, we are going to have a whole new way of communicating with the media. The guys who were in charge of that did a horrible job. The other side demonized Newt and made us into extremists. And we didn't do anything about it."

When the party's leaders found themselves losing the budget battle in the media, they admitted privately that the Democrats "were better at it," and they consoled themselves with the idea that "they [the Democrats] had been at it longer."[24] Gingrich's own amazing postmortem comment had a similarly defeatist tone. "We didn't think we were involved in a public relations game," he said.[25] And this from the acknowledged master of media manipulation during his insurgency phase. A contrast that reminds us again of the very different requirements of insurgency and governance.[26]

More broadly, these reactions remind us that in the forty years since the Republicans had governed, there had been a revolution in media involvement in the governing process. During those years it was the majority-party Democrats who cultivated the most media contacts, garnered the most publicity, and learned most from the experience. They learned to use the media to help support their legislative policymaking and to help win public confidence. That practice, what Timothy Cook calls "governing with the news" and "negotiating newsworthiness," was one more crucial political skill that the inexperienced new majority had not yet incorporated into its governing repertoire.[27]

As they campaigned (successfully) for reelection back home and looked forward to the 105th Congress, the two freshmen critiqued their own performance and, in so doing, revealed that the budget confrontation *had* taught them something about the legislative process. One said,

"As a member of a big class, I can tell you I was excited about the opportunity we had and I wanted to get everything at once. I thought this was our one big opportunity. Looking back, I think it was a mistake. We didn't need to get it all in one Congress, not even the balanced budget, the one thing I wanted to achieve more than anything else." The other one reported a similar lesson. "One change in my thinking that I haven't articulated for the papers is to be more incremental. If Clinton wins and we keep the House, we'll have to deal with him on his priorities and get what we want in bits and pieces." They had begun to entertain the realities of running the House under conditions of divided government.

The appreciation of these two freshmen for patient, step-by-step negotiation and for incremental progress shows they, and presumably their fellow newcomers, had learned something about governing. But the very elementary nature of their retrospectives also serves to underscore the initial inexperience that so crippled them during the 104th Congress. They had, indeed, needed some high school civics lessons. And the civics lessons of the budget confrontation had come at considerable cost—if not to them personally, then certainly to the new majority party.

IN THE IMMEDIATE sense, the cost to the Republicans was their failure to win a balanced budget agreement in the 104th Congress. In the long run, however, they failed because they did something few people thought could be done when they took over the Congress—they reelected President Bill Clinton to a second term.

When the budget process got under way, the president was adrift in the postelection doldrums, personally dispirited, politically down in the polls, on the losing side of the public debate, leader of a disorganized party, and widely thought to be a lame duck. Subsequent disclosures of the money-raising frenzy gripping the president and the White House in early 1995 were vivid reminders of his parlous condition. By the time his budget confrontation with the Republicans had run its course, however, he had been recharged with energy, reached his highest ever level in the polls, taken command of the political center, reshaped the public dialogue, revived the hopes of his party, and become a heavy favorite for reelection. The scope of that political transformation is mind-boggling and virtually impossible to pull off. But the Republicans had done it.

In his "near-death condition" the president had needed some outside event to give him an opportunity to reassert himself.[28] Republican all-or-nothing intransigence gave him that opportunity. And he took it. He vetoed some continuing resolutions; he picked popular budget priorities and threatened to veto any budget that compromised them; he spoke repeatedly of the need for "common ground."[29] He blamed the Republicans for the misery of the shutdown. And in the process he discovered a political label more politically punishing even than the label "liberal." That label was "extremist." By April, his approval rating stood at 56 percent, 21 points higher than that of Congress.[30]

In August, as the president rode the train to the Democratic National Convention in Chicago, one reporter wrote, "Yesterday, repeatedly and adamantly, Clinton bragged about his stand-off with Republicans over the budget."[31] A couple of days later, Al Gore brought a roaring convention to its feet. "They passed this reckless plan and they demanded that President Clinton sign it," he said.

> They shut the government down—twice, because they thought Bill Clinton would buckle under the pressure, wither in the face of attacks,

cave in to their demands. . . . [But] President Clinton took Speaker Newt Gingrich and Senator Bob Dole into the oval office. I was there, I remember. And he said, 'As long as I occupy this office, you will never enact this plan because as long as I am President, I will not let you.'[32]

The Republicans had helped him find a presidential voice. And that voice would keep him in office.

Not only did Republicans give aid and comfort to presidential candidate Bill Clinton, but the freshmen seemed to be a special handicap to their own candidate, Bob Dole. The very anti-Congress, anti-negotiation rhetoric they had used to win and to govern was picked up by Dole's Republican primary opponents Lamar Alexander and Pat Buchanan, who blasted the negotiation-minded Senate majority leader as being the epitome of everything wrong with the party. They in turn were blasted for what he called "calamitous political immaturity" by conservative columnist Charles Krauthammer, with the comment that "Republicans seem unable to realize they are no longer the party of protest, but the party of governance."[33]

The Democrats welcomed the Republican gift by linking Dole with "Newt Gingrich and the House freshman class."[34] "Dole's real problem in the election," wrote one analyst, is that "he got into the boat with Newt Gingrich and all those young congressmen."[35] For fear of their harmful effect on Dole's image, the freshman class was kept conspicuously under wraps at the Republican National Convention.[36] From beginning to end the freshman class was both a big part of the solution and a big part of the problem for the new governing majority.

After the election Dole's communications director acknowledged that "except for a few days of euphoria following the Republican convention, nothing ever changed from the day the Republicans closed down the government."[37] And as the president himself put it after his reelection, "The budget fight was a turning point."[38] For the Republicans, the shutdown strategy was a certifiable catastrophe. Their long-term goal of a unified conservative government—a Republican Congress and a Republican president—had been pushed further away than it had been two years before. That failure, I would argue, can be traced back in considerable part to their forty years in the minority and out of power in the House.

Speaker Gingrich's own postmortem confession illuminates the problem nicely. "I feel like a good Triple A player," he said, "who can't hit major league pitching."[39] His confrontational strategy was admirably suited to running an insurgency and leading the Republicans out of the political wilderness. But in the 104th Congress neither he nor his fellow partisans had a good grasp of what to do next—how to interpret their victory or how to govern the country.

FIVE

Beyond the 104th Congress

THE ARGUMENT of this essay extends only to the 104th Congress. It does not purport to prejudge or predict the performance of the 105th Congress. But because the Republicans retained their control of the House in the 1996 elections, the discussion invites our continuing attention to the learning curve of the House Republicans. Put differently, if one Congress is not time enough for a new majority to take hold after forty years out of power, how about two? Such, at least, are the questions posed by this analysis for students of the 105th Congress.

Near the end of the 104th, there was evidence—beyond that supplied by two freshmen—that some party-wide learning had taken place. Prodded by Senate bipartisanship, unnerved by their experience on the budget, and faced with an impending election, House Republicans participated in negotiating legislative enactments on minimum wage, drinking water, health insurance and, most important, welfare reform. Public approval of Congress improved.[1] And election analysts have argued that

this late-term conversion to compromise enabled the Republicans to preserve their House majority in the 1996
elections.[2] At the least their end-of-session performance
indicated an increased sensitivity to their reelection
needs. At the most, however, it may have marked the
beginning of a new governing strategy.

Early signs were mixed. In the immediate aftermath
of the elections, party leaders spoke of an "incrementalist" agenda for the 105th Congress.[3] And, accordingly,
they negotiated a give-and-take agreement with the president on a balanced budget plan. Further, Speaker Gingrich acknowledged that his radical party centralization
plan had not worked. For the future, he said,

> We need a slower, broader participatory struc-
> ture to move toward solving our problems. There
> will be a tremendous amount of implementation in
> this Congress and much less confrontation. And
> so I think that this kind of open leadership activity
> will work better than the centralized system.[4]

His prime-ministership adventure had ended, a victim
of experience. But his governing plans remained largely
experimental. In implementing the budgetary blueprint
he would now have to work out a new relationship with
the committee chairmen. And they, who had been rele-
gated to subcontractor status by his earlier plan, would
now have to learn how to manage their newfound influence.[5] Moreover, all of them together would have to work
out a new relationship with the minority party—in committee and on the floor.[6]

The indecisive, divided-government message of the
1996 elections did not provide any clear, strong guidance.
The Republicans failed to elect a president. They retained
control of the House, but barely, with the smallest majority in more than forty years.[7] Many of them had to
fight the election very much on the defensive: "I am not

Newt Gingrich." "We are not extremists." They neither sought nor gained an activating mandate. And despite what may have been an historic two-in-a-row success, they seem to have emerged from the election at least as disappointed and confused as energized and confident. In Speaker Gingrich's words, "The winning team *feels* defeated."[8] So, in spite of the budget agreement, it is hard to say whether or not the status quo election result helped to accelerate the development of a new governing strategy. We can conclude only that some learning had taken place and that some learning would have to continue.

An early reportorial effort to describe the postelection mood of the House majority in the new Congress suggested, in familiar terms, the need for continued learning. Describing the 1996 election as "a closer brush with disaster than is commonly realized," the authors found that "as a result [House Republicans] worry whether the ambitious Contract with America that guided them two years ago is the reason they retained power, or the reason they almost lost it."[9] In our story, the answer to that question is clear. The Contract was a major mistake legislatively, and it is part of the reason they almost lost power. Their continued devotion to the Contract is a kind of litmus test for House Republicans. To the extent that they look back on the Contract and its passage in the House as their finest legislative hour, they still have a lot to learn.

In the late spring of 1997 there was further indication of governing lessons yet unlearned. Faced with another highly publicized conflict with the president, the Republicans chose a showdown strategy eerily reminiscent of their disastrous budgetary performance in the 104th Congress, and with eerily similar results. As before, they precipitated the conflict by attaching unrelated and partisan items to a piece of important legislation. This time the vehicle was the multibillion-dollar aid package for the victims of the calamitous winter floods in the upper Midwest. The president promised a veto unless the riders were removed from the legislation. The Republicans refused to remove them and passed the bill. The president vetoed it. Public opinion, by an emotion-laden two-to-one margin blamed the Republican Congress for the impasse that was holding up help for the needy. Amid considerable public embarrassment and intraparty finger-pointing, the Republicans removed the riders and passed the bill.[10] Once again, they had to acknowledge a failed governing strategy—indeed, the very same confrontational strategy that had failed them two years earlier. Taking into account their negotiating success on the balanced budget blueprint and their negotiating failure on the disaster aid package, it would seem that the new majority party had not yet developed a consistent sense of what it means, and what it takes, to govern the country.

Shortly after the 1996 election, Minority Whip Tom DeLay declared flatly that "the last Congress is dead."[11] One implication was that we ought not to expect the problems of the 104th Congress to be visited upon the 105th. Another implication is that sufficient late-term and postelection learning had taken place to render the lessons of this essay irrelevant for thinking about the future. That may yet prove to be so. But the long-run developmental perspective of this essay argues against a hasty burial. After forty years in the minority, it seems very unlikely that a newly enfranchised majority party can establish a reasonably stable set of governing relationships inside— and outside—the institution in the space of one Congress or even two. A priori, therefore, and on the basis of scattered early evidence, it seems likely that many problems of the 104th Congress remained alive in the 105th. In which case it might be just as wise for the Republican leadership to revisit and reexamine the 104th Congress as to bury it. But answers to these questions of learning and governing will be found only in future performance.

IN CONCLUSION, I want to return to a larger institutional question. To the extent that the problems and mistakes of the new majority party can be explained by their forty years out of power, does this story suggest any normative judgments about forty years of one-party control of the House?

If we judge on purely partisan grounds, the answer is easy. Democrats will have one answer, Republicans another. If, however, we judge on institutional grounds, on the overall performance of a representative system of government, the answer is more complicated. My own earliest reaction to the 1994 congressional election was that it was the best thing that could have happened to this country in terms of the health of a representative system of government. On policy grounds, an occasional injection of new ideas into the system—the kind that comes with partisan turnover—seemed to me a good thing. It also seemed to me that on institutional grounds it is a good thing to give representatives of both parties some experience in governing and some sense for the responsibility and the accountability that comes with governing.

I did not foresee the ineptitude of the Republicans, which is one reason their problems fascinate me. In the beginning I believed that if they could win the election, they could probably govern. As it turned out, they couldn't. They couldn't interpret their victory or govern the country—not effectively or in their own long-term interest. I underestimated what I now argue is the very large impact that forty years out of power had on the incoming party. But that argument only strengthens my original conviction that an occasional alternation in party control is beneficial, while adding an updated conviction that forty years between such occasions is much too long for the system to reap those benefits.

For any new incoming majority, it may be that one term is just not enough time to recover from the effects of so many years in the minority. If that is true, then the newly empowered Republicans faced overwhelming odds, and we should be more sympathetic toward them than I have been. But it is not a matter of sympathy. It is a matter of institutional maintenance and institutional performance. The House as an institution neither looks well nor works well under the circumstances I have described.

One of the potential benefits from an alternation in party policy and party accountability in our most representative political institution is the opportunity it brings to refresh, enliven, and enhance our civic culture. The orderly, peaceful transfer of political power by free elections is, after all, the essential test of a functioning democracy. But the transfer of 1994 brought us very little civic renewal. Instead, we got an acceleration of partisan confrontation inside the institution and an acceleration of public distrust of Congress outside the institution. This outcome, I would argue, was in large measure due to the extreme length of time between changes in party control. In short, forty years of one-party rule was detrimental to our civic culture. And that impact could not be overcome easily or quickly.

We can certainly conclude that forty years without an alternation in party control of the House did not make it easy for the Republicans. But we might also conclude that forty years without an alternation in party control of that institution has not made it easy for the country either. From a normative standpoint, this second conclusion is a good deal more important than the first. And we ought not to wait for another forty years before we begin to worry about it.

Notes

Chapter One
Forty Years

1. Elizabeth Drew, "Can This Leadership Be Saved?" *Washington Post Weekly*, April 15–21, 1996.

2. Michael Weiskopf and David Maraniss, "Endgame: The Revolution Stalls," *Washington Post Weekly*, January 29–February 4, 1996.

3. A third very helpful book for understanding the ideological, antigovernment underpinnings of the Republican party, but again without an analysis of the institutional setting in Congress, is Dan Balz and Ronald Brownstein, *Storming the Gates* (Little, Brown, 1996).

Chapter Two
Electoral Interpretation and the
Majority-Minority Relationship

1. *Congressional Record*, daily ed., January 4, 1995, p. H4.

2. Barbara Sinclair, *Majority Party Leadership in the U.S. House* (Johns Hopkins University Press, 1983), p. 110.

3. Barbara Sinclair, *Legislators, Leaders and Lawmaking: The House of Representatives in the Post-Reform Era* (Johns Hopkins University Press, 1995), pp. 147, 304. See also Charles O. Jones, *Party and Policy Making: The House Republican Policy Committee* (Rutgers University Press, 1964), p. 136; and David Rohde, *Parties and Leaders in the Post-Reform House* (University of Chicago Press, 1991), p. 137.

4. Gary Cox and Matthew McCubbins, *Legislative Leviathan* (University of California Press, 1993), p. 2.

5. Roger Davidson and Walter Oleszek, *Congress against Itself* (Indiana University Press, 1977), pp. 67, 88, 137, 195, 208, 211, 240, 241, 251, 267; and David Rohde, "Electoral Forces, Political Agendas and Partisanship in the House and Senate," in Roger Davidson, ed., *The Post-Reform Congress* (St. Martins, 1992), pp. 27–47. On the Democratic culture permeating the committee system, see Ronald Peters, "The Republican Speakership," paper prepared for the 1996 annual meeting of the American Political Science Association.

6. Mickey Edwards, "A Tale of Two Reps: Study in Contrasts," *Boston Herald*, January 10, 1995. The Democrat was Dick Gephardt. The finest treatment, theoretically and historically, of these relationships between partisanship and procedure in Congress is Sarah Binder, *Minority Rights, Majority Rule* (Cambridge University Press, 1997).

7. See David Mayhew, "Congressional Elections: The Case of the Vanishing Marginals," *Polity*, vol. 6 (1974), pp. 295–318; Richard Born, "Generational Replacement and the Growth of Incumbent Reelection Margins in the U.S. House," *American Political Science Review*, vol. 73 (1979), pp. 811–17; Gary Jacobson, *The Electoral Origins of Divided Party Government* (Boulder, Colo.: Westview, 1990); Alan Ehrenhalt, *The United States of Ambition* (Random House, 1991); and John Gilmour and Paul Rothstein, "Early Republican Retirement: A Cause of Democratic Dominance in the House of Representatives," *Legislative Studies Quarterly*, vol. 18 (August 1993), pp. 345–65.

8. Juliana Greenwald and Deborah Kalb, "Poll Results Boost Hopes of Democrats," *Congressional Quarterly*, April 27, 1996.

9. Charles O. Jones, *The Minority Party in Congress* (Little, Brown, 1970), p. 170.

58 *Notes*

10. Jones, *Party and Policy Making*, p. 152. See also Burdett Loomis, *The New American Politicians* (Basic Books, 1988), p. 221.

11. William Connelly and John Pitney, *Congress' Permanent Minority? Republicans in the U.S. House* (Lanham, Md.: Little-field, Adams, 1994), p. 64.

12. Ibid., chap. 6; Richard Cohen, "Frustrated House Republicans Seek More Aggressive Strategy for 1984 and Beyond," *National Journal*, March 3, 1984; and Jeffrey Birnbaum, "House Republicans Frustrated in Minority Role Often Ask Themselves Whether It's Time to Leave," *Wall Street Journal*, June 5, 1987.

13. Richard Cohen, quoted in John Rhodes, "The Business of Being Minority Leader," *National Journal Quarterly*, November 29, 1977.

14. John Barry, *The Ambition and the Power* (Viking, 1989), p. 480.

15. Connelly and Pitney, *Congress' Permanent Minority?*, p. 69. See also Lloyd Grove, "An Elephant Never Forgets," *Washington Post*, November 28, 1994.

16. David Maraniss and Michael Weiskopf, *"Tell Newt To Shut Up!"* (Simon and Shuster, 1996), p. 31.

17. Quoted in Barry, *Ambition and the Power*, p. 482.

18. Quoted in Connelly and Pitney, *Congress' Permanent Minority?*, p. 86.

19. Ibid., p. 19.

20. Ibid., p. 62. The speaker was Tom DeLay, now majority whip.

21. Rohde, *Parties and Leaders*, chap. 1.

22. The struggles and the changes can be traced in Connelly and Pitney, *Congress' Permanent Minority?*; Jones, *Party and Policy Making*; Rohde, *Parties and Leaders*; Sinclair, *Legislators, Leaders and Lawmaking*; and in the running record of Newt Gingrich's public comments.

23. A thoughtful discussion of Gingrich in both institutional and personal terms is Randall Strahan, "Leadership in Institutional and Political Time: The Case of Newt Gingrich and the 104th Congress," paper prepared for the 1996 annual meeting of the American Political Science Association.

24. Irwin Arieff, "House Freshmen Republicans Seek Role as Power Brokers," *Congressional Quarterly*, July 7, 1979.

25. Connelly and Pitney, *Congress' Permanent Minority?*, p. 155.

26. Michael Barone, "Who Is This Newt Gingrich?," *Washington Post*, August 26, 1984.

27. Connelly and Pitney, *Congress' Permanent Minority?*, p. 27.

28. Peter Osterlund, "A Capitol Chameleon: What Will Newt Gingrich Do Next?," *Los Angeles Times*, August 25, 1991.

29. On Rhodes, see, for example, Richard Cohen, "House Republicans under Rhodes—Divided They Stand and Fret," *National Journal*, November 29, 1977; Arieff, "House Freshmen Republicans Seek Role as Power Brokers"; Mary Russell, "Low-Key Rhodes Woos Fired Up Freshmen and Conservatives," *Washington Post*, November 22, 1979; Mary Russell, "Rhodes Will Step Down as GOP Leader after Next Year," *Washington Post*, December 13, 1979; John Brummett, "Friend of Newt, Ex-Congressman Ed Bethune is 'Really Wired' Into The New GOP Power Loop," *Arkansas Democrat Gazette*, March 10, 1995; John Kolbe, "A Kinder, Gentler Congress: Rhodes Recounts More Civilized Age of DC Politics," *Arizona Republic*, December 17, 1995; and Michael Murphy and Kris Mayes, "Rhodes Lauds Gingrich Goals, But Finds Tactics Distasteful," *Arizona Republic*, October 14, 1995.

On Michel, see, for example, Martin Tolchin, "GOP Campaign: For House Leader," *New York Times*, September 28, 1980; Margot Hornblower, "Reps. Michel and VanderJagt Battling Fiercely to Lead House GOP," December 8, 1980; Margot Hornblower, "House GOP Picks Michel as Leader," *Washington Post*, December 9, 1980; Margot Hornblower, "The Master of Gentle Persuasion," *Washington Post*, August 10, 1981; David Broder, "Michel's Departure End of an Era," *Times Picayune*, October 12, 1993; Norman Ornstein, "Michel Exit Ends Era of Cooperative Republican Leaders," *Roll Call*, October 11, 1993; Robert Michel, remarks in *Congressional Record*, daily ed., November 29, 1994; and Janet Hook, "House Hones a Sharper Edge as Michel Turns in His Sword," *Congressional Quarterly*, October 9, 1993.

30. He even applied the same debilitating pressure to his party's leader, President George Bush. "You are killing us, you are just killing us," Bush told Gingrich when he fought Bush's budget compromise in 1990. Dan Balz and Serge Kovaleski, "Dividing the GOP, Conquering the Agenda," *Washington Post Weekly*, January 9–15, 1996.

31. Barry, *Ambition and the Power*, pp. 165–66.

32. Ibid., p. 688.

33. Connelly and Pitney, *Congress' Permanent Minority?*, p. 160.

34. Barry, *Ambition and the Power*, p. 366. See also p. 242.

35. David Rogers, "General Newt: GOP's Rare Year Owes Much to How Gingrich Disciplined the House," *Wall Street Journal*, December 18, 1995.

36. Representative Joseph Moakley, quoted in Jennifer Bradley and Ed Henry, "Members Bid Adieu to Historic 104th Congress," *Roll Call*, September 30, 1996.

37. Guy Gugliotta, "Which Way Did the Revolution Go?," *Washington Post Weekly*, March 10, 1997.

38. Osterlund, "Capitol Chameleon." See also Rohde, *Parties and Leaders*, p. 129.

39. Connelly and Pitney, *Congress' Permanent Minority?* p. 160.

40. Jackie Koszczuk, "Gingrich Struggling to Control Revolts among the Troops," *Congressional Quarterly*, December 23, 1995, p. 3865.

41. A different, more extensively developed, and very helpful view of Gingrich is Ronald Peters, "The Republican Speakership," paper prepared for the 1996 annual meeting of the American Political Science Association.

Chapter Three

Governing: The Contract, the Freshmen, the Speaker

1. Karen Hosler, "GOP Gets a Glimpse of the Promised Land," *Baltimore Sun*, May 14, 1995.

2. John Harwood, "Reagan-Era Veterans Are Now Determined to Revive '80s Policies," *Wall Street Journal*, January 4, 1995.

3. George Hager and Eric Pianin, *Mirage* (Random House, 1997), pp. 255–58; John Aldrich and David Rohde, "The Republican Revolution and the House Appropriations Committee," paper prepared for the 1996 annual meeting of the Southern Political Science Association; and David Cloud and Jackie Koszczuk, "GOP's All-or-Nothing Approach Hangs on a Balanced Budget," *Congressional Quarterly*, December 9, 1995.

4. Jeff Shear, "Force Majeure?," *National Journal*, March 11, 1995.

5. Paul Taylor and Helen Dewar, "Outsiders on the Inside," *Washington Post Weekly*, July 17–23, 1995.

5. Robin Toner, "73 Mr. Smiths, of the GOP, Go to Washington," *New York Times*, January 7, 1995.

7. David Brady and Naomi Lynn, "Switched Seat Congressional Districts: Their Effects on Party Voting and Public Policy," *American Journal of Political Science*, vol. 17 (August 1973); Patricia Hurley, David Brady, and Joseph Cooper, "Measuring Legislative Potential for Policy Change," *Legislative Studies Quarterly*, vol. 11 (November 1977); David Brady, "Critical Elections, Congressional Parties and Clusters of Policy Change," *British Journal of Political Science*, vol. 8 (January 1978). For an argument that the size of the freshman class in the majority party brings rules changes, see Scott Ainsworth, Patrick Fett, and Itai Sened, "The Implications of Turnover and Term Limits on Institutional Stability," *American Journal of Political Science*, forthcoming.

8. Shear, "Force Majeure?"

9. Toner, "73 Mr. Smiths"; Kevin Merida and Kenneth Cooper, "A Class of Young Warriors," *Washington Post Weekly*, December 12–25, 1994; Graeme Browning, "The GOP's Young Turks," *National Journal*, February 25, 1995; Jackie Koszczuk, "Freshmen: New Powerful Voice," *Congressional Quarterly*, October 28, 1995; and Cohen, "The Transformers," *National Journal*, March 4, 1995.

10. Shear, "Force Majeure?" ; Guy Gugliotta, "They Flat Do Not Care," *Washington Post Weekly*, January 1–7, 1996; Rhodes Cook, "Republican Freshmen Voting Support . . ."; and Karen

Hosler, "Humbled House Freshmen Regroup," *Baltimore Sun*, January 26, 1996.

11. Susan Feeney, "GOP Presidential Candidates Prize Nod from House Freshmen," *Dallas Morning News*, January 17, 1996.

12. Toner, "73 Mr. Smiths."

13. Jim Mann, "Mission to Balkans; House Freshmen Cut Foreign Policy Class," *Los Angeles Times*, December 2, 1995.

14. Jill Zuckman, "GOP Freshmen Drive Debate in Washington," *Boston Globe*, October 22, 1995.

15. Jerry Gray, "Grading GOP Freshmen: High in Ambition, Low in Humility," *New York Times*, April 11, 1995.

16. Gugliotta, "They Flat Do Not Care."

17. Rhodes Cook, "Can GOP Freshmen Make Comeback?," *Congressional Quarterly*, June 29, 1996.

18. Gray, "Grading GOP Freshmen."

19. Browning, "GOP's Young Turks."

20. Toner, "73 Mr. Smiths"; and Merida and Cooper, "Class of Young Warriors."

21. Merida and Cooper, "Class of Young Warriors."

22. Browning, "GOP's Young Turks."

23. Randall Strahan, "Leadership in Institutional and Political Time: The Case of Newt Gingrich and the 104th Congress," paper prepared for the 1996 annual meeting of the American Political Science Association; and Rogers, "General Newt."

24. John Owens, "The Return of Party Government in the U.S. House of Representatives: Central Leadership-Committee Relations in the 104th Congress," *British Journal of Political Science*, vol. 27 (April 1997), pp. 247–72.

25. Roger Davidson, "Building a Republican Regime on Capitol Hill," in Lawrence C. Dodd, ed., *Extension of Remarks*, Legislative Studies section, American Political Science Association, December 1995; John Aldrich and David Rohde, "Conditional Party Government Revisited: Majority Party Leadership and the Committee System in the 104th Congress," in Dodd, ed., *Extension of Remarks*; Strahan, "Leadership in Institutional and Political Time"; Owens, "Return of Party Government"; Peters, "Republican Speakership"; C. Lawrence Evans and Walter J. Oleszek, "Partisan Leadership and Committee Reform," papers prepared for the 1996 annual meeting of the American Political Science Association; John H. Aldrich and

David W. Rohde, "The Republican Revolution and the House Appropriations Committee," working paper 96–08, Institute for Public Policy and Social Research, Michigan State University, 1996. See also David S. Cloud, "Speaker Wants His Platform to Rival the Presidency," *Congressional Quarterly*, February 4, 1995; and David Rogers and Phil Funtz, "How Gingrich Grabbed Power and Attention–and His New Risks," *Wall Street Journal*, January 1, 1995.

26. David Rohde, *Parties and Leaders in the Post-Reform House* (University of Chicago Press, 1991); and Aldrich and Rohde, "Republican Revolution."

27. Ronald Peters, *The American Speakership* (Johns Hopkins University Press, 1990), pp. 201, 207.

28. Burdett Loomis, *The New American Politicians* (Basic Books, 1988); and Roger Davidson, ed., *The Post-Reform Congress* (St. Martins, 1992).

29. Jill Zuckman, "Freshmen Keep House on Course to the Right," *Boston Globe*, February 26, 1995.

30. Richard Fenno, *Home Style: House Members in Their Districts* (Little, Brown, 1978), pp. 162–69.

31. Dan Balz and Serge Kovaleski, "Dividing the GOP, Conquering the Agenda," *Washington Post Weekly*, January 9–15, 1996.

32. Tim Barnett and Burdett Loomis, "The 104th Republicans: of Classes and Cannon Fodder," in Burdett Loomis, ed., *Extension of Remarks*, Legislative Studies section, American Political Science Association, January 1997.

33. David Broder, "Keeping the GOP Juggernaut on Track," *Washington Post Weekly*, July 24–30, 1995.

34. James Gimpel, *Fulfilling the Contract: The First 100 Days* (Boston: Allyn and Bacon, 1996), pp. 46–47.

35. Jessica Lee, "New Course for GOP Freshmen," *USA Today*, January 30, 1995.

36. David Rogers, "Congress and White House Agree to Buy Time, But Gingrich Says, Budget Pact Must Come Soon," *Wall Street Journal*, October 2, 1995.

37. Zuckman, "GOP Freshmen Drive Debate."

38. Morton Kondracke, *Roll Call*, December 18, 1995. See also David Rogers,, "In Budget Impasse, Gingrich's Control over GOP Rank and File is Never Clear," *Wall Street Journal*,

November 16, 1995; and Koszczuk, "Freshmen: New, Powerful Voice."

Chapter Four
The Budget Confrontation and Its Aftermath

1. The story of the conflict has been admirably told by others. I have relied on them heavily for the facts, not for the interpretations. See George Hager and Eric Pianin, *Mirage* (Random House, 1997); Hedrick Smith (narrator) "The Elected: The Presidency and Congress," part of the series, *The People and the Power Game*, Public Broadcasting System, August 1996, pp. 9–92; Elizabeth Drew, *Showdown: The Struggle between the Gingrich Congress and the Clinton White House* (Simon and Schuster, 1996); and David Maraniss and Michael Weiskopf, *"Tell Newt to Shut Up!"* (Simon and Schuster, 1996).

2. David Rogers, "GOP's Rare Year Owes Much to How Gingrich Disciplined the House," *Wall Street Journal*, December 18, 1995.

3. Hager and Pianin, *Mirage*, pp. 14–19; and Maraniss and Weiskopf, *"Tell Newt to Shut Up!,"* p. 38.

4. Jackie Calmes, "Fight over the Balanced Budget Could Prove to Be Defining Moment for Gingrich and His Agenda," *Wall Street Journal*, December 6, 1995.

5. George Hager, "Budget Battle Came Sooner Than Either Side Expected," *Congressional Quarterly*, November 18, 1995.

6. David Rogers, "Congress and White House Agree to Buy Time, But Gingrich Says Budget Pact Must Come Soon," *Wall Street Journal*, October 2, 1995.

7. Calmes, "Fight over the Balanced Budget."

8. Hager, "Budget Battle." On the genesis and the effect of the rider, see Hager and Pianin, *Mirage*, pp. 259–60.

9. John Young, ". . . And the Small: Gingrich Wants His Place in the Sun," *Washington Post Weekly*, November 20–26, 1995.

10. David Cloud and Jackie Koszczuk, "GOP's All-or-Nothing Approach Hangs on a Balanced Budget," *Congressional Quarterly*, December 9, 1995.

11. Hager and Pianin, *Mirage*, p. 244.

12. Smith, "The Elected: The Presidency and Congress."

13. For example, Dan Morgan, "Redefining the Word 'Budget,'" *Washington Post Weekly*, August 21–27, 1995; Julianna Gruenwald, "GOP Freshmen Are Determined to Defy One Term Tradition," *Congressional Quarterly*, October 28, 1995; David Wessel, "Budget Battle Hides Congressional Victories That Reduce Spending," *Wall Street Journal*, November 11, 1995; Hager and Pianin, *Mirage*, esp. pp. 252, 263; David Rogers, "General Newt: GOP's Rare Year Owes Much to How Gingrich Disciplined the House, *Wall Street Journal*, December 18, 1995"; Jackie Calmes and David Rogers, "Historic Budget Battle Ends with a Whimper as Congress Wraps Up Work on Spending Deal," *Wall Street Journal*, April 26, 1996; and Jonathan Weisman, "True Impact on GOP Congress Reaches Well Beyond Bills," *Congressional Quarterly*, September 7, 1996.

14. Maraniss and Weiskopf, *"Tell Newt to Shut Up!,"* chap. 11; and Hager and Pianin, *Mirage*, pp. 264–69.

15. See the comment by Robert Reischauer in George Hager, "Clinton's Budget: Trying to Balance His Goals," *Congressional Quarterly*, March 23, 1996.

16. Smith, "The Elected: The Presidency and Congress."

17. Ibid.

18. Charles E. Cook, "Lack of Leadership, Followership Produces House GOP Paralysis," *Roll Call*, March 11, 1996.

19. Stephen Greene, "GOP Freshmen Acting as Budget Conscience," *San Diego Union Tribune*, December 23, 1995.

20. Jill Zuckman, "GOP Freshmen Drive Debate in Washington," *Boston Globe*, October 22, 1995.

21. Guy Gugliotta, "They Flat Do Not Care," *Washington Post Weekly*, January 1–7, 1996.

22. Jackie Koszczuk, "Freshmen: New, Powerful Voice," *Congressional Quarterly*, October 28, 1995. CBO scoring refers to the numerical estimates and projections of yearly government spending, revenues, interest, and deficit produced by the Congressional Budget Office.

23. Smith, "The Elected: The Presidency and Congress."

24. Maraniss and Weiskopf, *"Tell Newt to Shut Up!,"* p. 166.

25. Ann Scales, "Gingrich Faults Handling of '94 Takeover," *Boston Globe*, June 27, 1996.

26. For Gingrich as an accomplished media manipulator in his insurgency phase, see Katharine Seelye, "Gingrich First Mastered the Media, and Then Rose to Be King of the Hill," *New York Times*, December 14, 1994; and Howard Kurtz, "How to Really Work the Press," *Washington Post Weekly*, April 3–9, 1995.

27. Timothy Cook, *Governing with the News* (University of Chicago Press, 1997); and Cook, "The Negotiation of Newsworthiness," in Ann N. Crigler, ed., *The Psychology of Political Communication* (University of Michigan Press, 1996). In her pre-1994 study Karen Kedrowski found that House Democrats were more likely to be "media entrepreneurs" than House Republicans. Karen Kedrowski, *Media Entrepreneurs and the Media Enterprise in the U.S. Congress* (Cresskill, N.J.: Hampton Press, 1996). For the learning problem of the majority leader, see Jerry Gray, "The Speaker's Gruff No. 2 Takes Charge in the House," *New York Times*, April 1, 1996.

28. Rhodes Cook, "Clinton Rides Timely Surge to Chicago," *Congressional Quarterly*, August 17, 1996.

29. David Wessel and Jackie Calmes, "With Autumn Shutdown of Government Coming, Maneuvering by Clinton and the GOP Is Intense," *Wall Street Journal*, July 25, 1995; and Dan Balz and Ronald Brownstein, *Storming the Gates* (Little, Brown, 1996), p. 353.

30. *Gallup Poll Monthly*, April 1996.

31. Brian McGrory, "From Back of Train, Clinton Takes Race Forward," *Boston Globe*, August 26, 1996.

32. Convention Speech, *Congressional Quarterly*, August 31, 1996.

33. Charles Krauthammer, "GOP Lacks Maturity to Govern," *Rochester Democrat and Chronicle*, February 25, 1996.

34. Dan Balz and David Broder, "Inside the GOP Campaign," *Washington Post Weekly*, April 27–28, 1996.

35. Phil Joyce, "Looking at Snapshots of Bob Dole," *Philadelphia Inquirer*, October 12, 1996.

36. David Rogers and Dennis Farney, "Week in the Sun Gives GOP a Whole New Attitude," *Wall Street Journal*, August 16, 1996; and Michael Rezendes, "For First Term Class, Unhappy Initiation," *Boston Globe*, August 16, 1996.

37. Mary McGrory, "Dole Returned to Civility after Defeat," *Rochester Democrat and Chronicle*, November 8, 1996.

38. Alison Mitchell, "Stung by Defeats in '94, Clinton Regrouped and Coopted GOP Policies," *New York Times*, November 7, 1996. See also, John Harris, "The Keys to the White House," *Washington Post Weekly*, November 11–17, 1996; and Michael Frisby, "How Clinton Revived a Campaign Once Seen as Hopeless," *Wall Street Journal*, November 6, 1996.

39. Adam Clymer, "Firebrand Who Got Singed Says Being Speaker Suffices," *New York Times*, January 22, 1996. See also his earlier confession that "I had always looked at becoming Speaker intellectually. Living it is a different experience." "Gingrich Dazed by Debut, Relishes Battle," *Rochester Democrat and Chronicle*, April 9, 1995; and E. J. Dionne Jr. ". . . And the Pugnacious Past Is a Problem," *Boston Globe*, September 15, 1996.

Chapter Five
Beyond the 104th Congress

1. Gary Jacobson, "Congress: Unprecedented and Unsurprising," in Michael Nelson, ed., *The Elections of 1996* (Washington: CQ Press, 1997), p. 161.

2. Ibid; Helen Dewar and Eric Pianin, "Choosing Pragmatism over Partisanship," *Washington Post Weekly*, August 12–18, 1996; and Dewar and Pianin, "A Switch in Time That May Have Saved the GOP," *Washington Post Weekly*, October 7–13, 1996.

3. "GOP Outlines Plan for '97," *Rochester Democrat and Chronicle*, November 26, 1996.

4. Damon Chappie, "GOP Changes Style, But Not Its Leadership," *Roll Call*, November 21, 1996.

5. On the 104th Congress see Juliet Eilperin, "House Bills Bypass Committee Process," *Roll Call*, March 18, 1996. On the 105th see Charles Cook, "The Onus to Beat 'Do Nothing' Rap Falls to Chairmen," *Roll Call*, May 12, 1997. For early suggestions that the new Congress had "reverted to form" see Ronald

Elving, "Fireworks of 104th Now a Faint Glow," *Congressional Quarterly*, March 8, 1997.

6. For some early indications of Republican party learning—their reconsideration their ban on proxy voting in committee and their use of open rules on the floor—see Gabriel Kahn, "GOP to Rethink Proxy Voting Ban," *Roll Call*, June 26, 1995; and "How to Stifle Debate," *Roll Call*, March 18, 1996.

7. Rhodes Cook, "Freshman Job Security No Comfort for GOP," *Congressional Quarterly*, February 27, 1997; and Christopher Georges, "Backbone of GOP Agenda May Be Crumbling under the Strain of Freshman Reelection Races," *Wall Street Journal*, March 1, 1996.

8. Dan Balz and John Yang, "Republicans Set Legislative Priorities," *Washington Post Weekly*, March 7, 1997. The historical lesson will be found in Jacobson, "Congress: Unprecedented and Unsurprising."

9. Gerald Seib and Carla Anne Robbins, "Republicans Do Battle against One Another over Numerous Issues," *Wall Street Journal*, April 14, 1997.

10. David Rogers, "Congress Votes $8.9 Billion in Disaster Aid," *Wall Street Journal*, June 13, 1997. See also material on the front page and editorial page of the same date.

11. Chappie, "GOP Changes Style."

Index